THE OFFICIAL
MANCHESTER CITY
ANNUAL 2016

A Grange Publication

© 2015 Published by Grange Communications Ltd., Edinburgh, under licence from Manchester City Football Club. Printed in the EU.

Every effort has been made to ensure the accuracy of information within this publication but the publishers cannot be held responsible for any errors or omissions. Views expressed are those of the author and do not necessarily represent those of the publishers or the football club. All rights reserved.

Written by David Clayton
Designed by Simon Thorley

Photographs © MCFC (thanks to Sharon Latham and Victoria Haydn)

ISBN: 978-1-910199-49-7

D0682367

Contents

SEASON REVIEW 2014/15

Our month-by-month guide to City's season...

AUGUST

The campaign began in disappointing fashion as City lost the FA Community Shield 3-0 to Arsenal at Wembley, but with a number of players missing due to the World Cup in Brazil, it was far from the Blues' strongest squad.

A week later City travelled to Newcastle for the opening game of the Premier League season and though Alan Pardew's side put up a decent fight, goals from David Silva and a late second from Sergio Aguero ensured the champions started the 2014/15 campaign in the best possible fashion.

Manuel Pellegrini's men then comfortably saw off Liverpool with a 3-1 win at the Etihad Stadium over the team who pushed City so hard for the title the previous season. Stevan Jovetic (2) and Aguero were the scorers, and with confidence high and the goals flowing, more of the same was expected against Stoke City. But the Potters stunned everyone by leaving with a 1-0 victory, the Blues were very disappointing on the day. It was the first sign that there may be one or two problems ahead.

August record (all comps): Played: 4 Won: 2 Drawn: 0 Lost: 2 Goals for: 5 Goals against: 5

Etihad Player of the Month: Stevan Jovetic

SEPTEMBER

City faced Arsenal for the second time in little more than a month after the September international break. In an entertaining game, the Blues went ahead through Sergio Aguero but had to rely on a late equaliser from Martin Demichelis to earn a 2-2 draw. This was followed by the opening Champions League group game away to Bayern Munich – a game the Germans won 1-0.

The month didn't get any easier with Chelsea up next at the Etihad and, trailing 1-0 with Pablo Zabaleta sent off, it looked as though City would suffer another disappointment until substitute Frank Lampard equalised against his former club with just five minutes remaining to earn a 1-1 draw.

The Blues returned to winning ways three days later with a 7-0 victory over Sheffield Wednesday in the Capital One Cup thanks to goals from Lampard (2), Edin Dzeko (2), Jesus Navas, Yaya Toure and Jose Pozo.

The goals continued to flow with a thrilling 4-2 win away to Hull City. Aguero and Dzeko put City 2-0 up after just 11 minutes, but the Tigers fought back to level the scores and it took a 68th-minute goal from Dzeko and another from Lampard to settle the match. Lampard and Dzeko had both bagged four goals during September and a busy month ended with a 1-1 Champions League draw with Roma at the Etihad – Aguero scoring from the spot for City.

September record (all comps):
Played: 6 Won: 2 Drawn: 3 Lost: 1 Goals for: 15 Goals against: 5
Etihad Player of the Month: Frank Lampard

OCTOBER

With the goals flowing again, City started October with a 2-0 win away to Aston Villa with Yaya Toure and Aguero scoring in the last ten minutes of the game. Then Aguero moved into double figures for the season when he scored all four goals as the Blues thrashed Spurs 4-1 with a win at the Etihad. Later he was on target again in a 2-2 draw with CSKA. The result in Russia left City without a win in their opening three group games and facing an uphill task to qualify for the knock-out stages.

October got worse, with a 2-1 defeat at West Ham in the Premier League followed by the end of the Capital One Cup defence with a shock 2-0 home loss to Newcastle United. Things had to improve and quickly!

October record (all comps): Played: 5 Won: 2 Drawn: 1 Lost: 2 Goals for: 9 Goals against: 7
Etihad Player of the Month: Sergio Aguero

NOVEMBER

City began November in the best possible style with Aguero's 63rd-minute goal giving the Blues a 1-0 win over Manchester United. The victory kept City in third place, six points behind leaders Chelsea and with a vital game against CSKA Moscow up next, Pellegrini's side were in good heart going into a game that would hopefully put their Champions League dreams back on course. Instead, City were losing with just 100 seconds on the clock and despite Yaya Toure's equaliser, eventually went down 2-1 with Yaya and Fernandinho both being shown red cards. That seemed to be the end of City's hopes with Bayern Munich and Roma still to play. A 2-2 draw at QPR (Aguero scoring twice) hardly lifted the gloom three days later but goals from Stevan Jovetic and Toure secured a 2-1 win over Swansea after an international break. The Blues followed that up with a dramatic 3-2 win over Bayern Munich with Aguero scoring twice in the final five minutes to complete his hat-trick and give his team a glimmer of hope of progressing to the Round of 16. An impressive 3-0 victory away to Southampton (Toure, Lampard, Gael Clichy) put the champions back to second and ended the month on a high.

November record (all comps): Played: 6 Won: 4 Drawn: 1 Lost: 1 Goals for: 12 Goals against: 7
Etihad Player of the Month: Sergio Aguero

DECEMBER

City's scintillating form continued at the start of December with a stunning 4-1 win away to Sunderland – a venue the Blues rarely leave with anything other than a 1-0 loss. Aguero scored goals 18 and 19 for the campaign, and Jovetic and Zabaleta were also on target as the champions continued to chase down Chelsea. But the next game, a 1-0 win over Everton, came at a great cost with Aguero limping off after only a few minutes with a knee injury, just when the Argentine had been in the form of his life. Toure's penalty settled the game but the loss of Kun was just the beginning of a striker crisis.

The Blues produced a superb display in their final Champions' League group game, beating AS Roma in Italy thanks to goals from Samir Nasri and Zabaleta, to qualify for the Round of 16 and make it six wins in succession. It seemed City had finally found the momentum and sparkle missing earlier in the season and a 1-0 win at Leicester courtesy of Frank Lampard continued the feel-good factor. The last game before Christmas saw City – missing strikers Aguero, Dzeko and Jovetic – triumph 3-0 over Crystal Palace with two goals from Silva and another from Toure, and a sparkling 3-1 win over West Brom on Boxing Day (Fernando, Toure and Silva) put the Blues within touching distance of Chelsea.

Nine wins in a row – the champions looked determined to defend their crown and the final game of 2014 offered the opportunity to make it a perfect ten wins on the bounce. Goals from Silva and Fernandinho put City 2-0 up on 33 minutes, but Burnley fought back to draw 2-2 to stun the Etihad crowd.

December record (all comps): Played: 7 Won: 6 Drawn: 1 Lost: 0 Goals for: 16 Goals against: 3

Etihad Player of the Month: David Silva

JANUARY

A hard-fought 3-2 win over Sunderland (Toure, Jovetic and Lampard) finally saw City draw level at the top with Chelsea – though the sides' identical record meant the West London side remained in pole position for alphabetical reasons only! The FA Cup proved a welcome distraction, though the fact Sheffield Wednesday were again drawn to play at the Etihad was a little odd. Two James Milner goals proved enough to secure a 2-1 win, but the Blues, who would now be without Toure and new signing Wilfried Bony for the next six weeks due to Ivory Coast duty, were wobbling a little. Fernandinho opened the scoring in the next game away to Everton, but City were forced to settle for a 1-1 draw after conceding a 78th-minute equaliser to Naismith and Chelsea opened up a two-point lead at the top. It was the start of a poor spell for the champions, who would steadily fall behind Jose Mourinho's side in the next few weeks. A disappointing 2-0 home loss to Arsenal and a home FA Cup exit to Middlesbrough made for a miserable few weeks for City fans, and despite a respectable 1-1 draw at Chelsea (Silva), a win was really needed to close the gap at the top.

January record (all comps): Played: 6 Won: 2 Drawn: 2 Lost: 2 Goals for: 7 Goals against: 9 Etihad Player of the Month: James Milner

FEBRUARY

City were, again, well-below par for the home game with Hull City and trailed 1-0 going into injury time. But Milner's last-gasp free-kick earned a 1-1 draw that, in real terms, was two more points dropped. A 4-1 win away to Stoke saw the fit-again Aguero score his first goals in six games. Kun struck twice and further efforts from Nasri and Milner completed the rout.

The Blues followed that with an emphatic 5-0 win over Newcastle United at the Etihad. Aguero, Nasri, Dzeko and Silva (2) scored to put Pellegrini's side in great heart for the Round of 16 clash with Barcelona, but Luis Suarez came back to haunt the Blues as he scored twice in a 2-1 first leg victory. Aguero's second-half goal and Joe Hart's injury time penalty save from Lionel Messi gave City a glimmer of hope, but no more than that.

February record (all comps): Played: 4 Won: 2 Drawn: 1 Lost: 1 Goals for: 11 Goals against: 4 Etihad Player of the Month: David Silva

MARCH

City went into March knowing they couldn't afford anymore slip-ups, but away to Liverpool, two stunning goals from Henderson and Coutinho sealed a 2-1 defeat. Dzeko had earlier equalised and Chelsea's lead at the top – five points plus a game in hand – was suddenly looking ominous.

Goals from Silva and Milner secured a 2-0 midweek win over Leicester City, but a galling 1-0 loss to Burnley at Turf Moor was a further massive blow. Despite a gutsy display in the Nou Camp, the Blues were beaten 1-0 by Barcelona to end interest in the Champions League for another season, and there was by now an acceptance that retaining the title would be unlikely. The Blues ended the month a 3-0 win over West Brom with Bony, Fernando and Silva on target, but it would take a minor miracle to catch leaders Chelsea, who still looked very comfortable at the top with a six-point advantage and a game in hand.

**March record (all comps): Played: 5 Won: 2
Drawn: 0 Lost: 3 Goals for: 6 Goals against: 4
Etihad Player of the Month: Joe Hart**

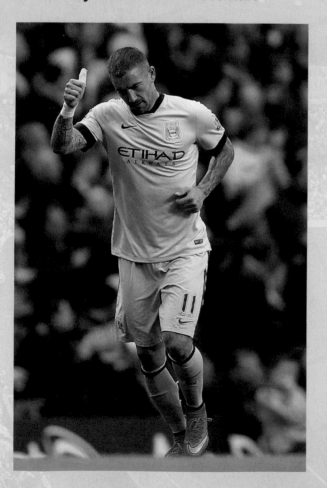

APRIL

While City still believed, a 2-1 loss at Crystal Palace meant even the most optimistic Blues conceded the title was heading for Stamford Bridge. Yaya Toure scored City's only goal, but there was now a further problem for the Blues who had slipped to fourth in the table. Worse still, Aguero's two goals that took him to a century in the Manchester derby were in vain as City were well beaten 4-2 at Old Trafford meaning Pellegrini's side now had a fight on their hands to qualify for the Champions League. It would take a steely resolve to end the campaign strongly, but that's what City did. Back-to-back Etihad wins - 2-0 over West Ham (Collins' own-goal and Aguero) and an entertaining 3-2 win over Aston Villa (Aguero, Kolarov and Fernandinho) - ended April and put City back up to second.

**April record: Played: 4 Won: 2 Drawn: 0
Lost: 2 Goals for: 7 Goals against: 8
Etihad Player of the Month: Sergio Aguero**

MAY

City ended the 2014/15 season on a high, winning the final four games. Aguero's winner at Spurs secured a 1-0 win before QPR were dispatched 6-0 at the Etihad. Aguero scored his third hat-trick of the season against the Hoops and there were also goals for Kolarov, Milner and Silva. The last road trip saw City beat Swansea 4-2 at The Liberty Stadium with Toure (2), Milner and Bony on target. That was followed by a 2-0 win over Southampton that proved to be a special day for many reasons. Lampard scored in his final Premier League game before moving to New York City FC, Joe Hart's clean sheet won him the Golden Glove award and Aguero's late strike secured the Golden Boot for ending as the Premier League's top scorer. The Blues finished runners-up and ended the campaign with their heads held high.

May record: Played: 4 Won: 4 Drawn: 2 Lost: 2 Goals for: 13 Goals against: 2

Training Ground funnies

The players enjoying themselves during training – this is what they might have said...

01

PROOF THAT GOALKEEPERS ARE REALLY FRUSTRATED SWEEPERS...

02

ZABA TAKES TEETH FLOSSING TO A WHOLE NEW LEVEL...

SERGIO SCARES HIMSELF WITH HIS NEW FINGERLESS GLOVES – "WHERE'VE THEY GONE!?" IT'S OK, HE FOUND THEM IN THE END...

04

OK, WHO'S TAKEN MY SHORTS?

New Signing#1

RAHEEM**STERLING**

Exciting winger/attacking midfielder/forward Raheem Sterling became City's record signing, as well as the most expensive English player ever, when he joined the Blues in the summer.

Skilful, speedy and strong, he is regarded as one of the brightest young talents in English football.

The 20-year-old joined City from Liverpool, having earned a reputation as one of Europe's hottest talents over the past two seasons.

Sterling, who opted for the No.7 shirt for the 2015/16 season, began his career at Queens Park Rangers before joining Liverpool as a 15-year-old in 2010 for an initial fee of £600,000.

He made his debut aged 17 against Wigan Athletic in 2012, and went on to make 129 appearances for the Reds, scoring 23 goals.

In 2014 he became only the second English player to win the Golden Boy award – an honour bestowed by European sports journalists on the Under-21 player that has had the most impressive season – with previous winners including Lionel Messi, Sergio Aguero, Isco and Paul Pogba – not bad company to be in.

A 2015 professional study by research group Soccerex rated Sterling as the most valuable young player in Europe. He also won back-to-back Liverpool FC Young Player of the Year awards for the 2013/14 and 2014/15 campaigns.

Born in Jamaica, Sterling moved to London at the age of seven and was inspired to become a footballer because of the family home's proximity to Wembley Stadium. After catching the eye of scouts at a junior level, he was snapped up by Queens Park Rangers' academy.

He spent seven years at Loftus Road, and during his time with the Hoops made his international debut at under-16 level with England. He then made the move to Merseyside to join Liverpool in 2010, where he made a name for himself as one of the country's rising stars.

A string of impressive displays for the Reds earned him the Golden Boy award in 2014, when a panel of sports journalists dubbed him the best player under the age of 21 playing in Europe. During his time at Anfield, Sterling also became the youngest ever Liverpool player to receive an international cap.

Since then he has continued to develop, becoming a star for both club and country. Having joined City, he hopes to help the club challenge for more silverware. An exciting signing!

Name: Raheem Sterling **Position:** Attacking midfielder **Squad Number:** 7
Date of Birth: 8/12/1994 **Previous Clubs:** QPR, Liverpool

2014/15 Appearances (All Comps): 0* 2014/15 Goals (All Comps): 0
Total City career: Played: 0 | Goals: 0 | (*with City)

BORN: Sterling was born on 8th December 1994 in Kingston, Jamaica. He moved to London aged 7, when his family emigrated to St Raphael's estate, Wembley. He attended Copland School.

SCOUTED: Raheem was scouted by veteran youth team coach Tom Whalley. When Whalley spotted Sterling playing with jumpers for goalposts, he put him through a strenuous running routine to test his character.

2003 -2010: During this time he played for Queens Park Rangers, featuring regularly for the U-18s.

27TH FEB 2010: Sterling joined Liverpool as a 15-year-old for an initial fee of £600,000.

1ST AUGUST 2010: This was Sterling's first appearance for the first team in a pre-season friendly in Germany against Borussia Monchengladbach.

14TH FEB 2011: Whilst playing for the youth team, Sterling scored five goals in a 9-0 win over Southend United.

24TH MARCH 2012: Sterling made his senior Liverpool debut as a substitute in a League match against Wigan Athletic aged 17 years.

AUGUST 2012: He made his European debut for the club, coming on as a substitute in a UEFA Europa League tie.
The following week he scored his first goal for the senior team in a friendly against Bayer Leverkusen.

20TH OCT 2012: Sterling scored his first senior competitive goal for Liverpool in a 1-0 win against Reading, making him the second youngest player ever to score in a competitive fixture for Liverpool behind Michael Owen.

14TH NOV 2012: He made his senior debut for England in a friendly away to Sweden.

21ST DEC 2012: Sterling signed a contract extension that committed his future to Liverpool.

27TH AUG 2013: He scored his first goal of the 2013-14 season, and the opening goal against Notts County, in a 4-2 win in the League Cup.

4TH DEC 2013: Sterling scored his first Premier League goal of the season for Liverpool in a 5-1 win over Norwich City.

13TH APRIL 2014: Sterling scored two goals and assisted another as Liverpool won 3-2 over Manchester City.

12TH MAY 2014: He was named in England's 23-man squad for the 2014 FIFA World Cup.

14TH DEC 2014: He made his 100th appearance for Liverpool in a match against Manchester United.

20TH DEC 2014: Sterling was named as the recipient of the 2014 Golden Boy Award.

27TH MARCH 2015: Sterling scored his first senior goal for England in a 4-0 UEFA Euro 2016 qualifier against Lithuania.

19TH MAY 2015: He was named Liverpool's 'Young Player of the Season'.

12TH JULY 2015: Liverpool confirms that a record-breaking agreement has been reached with Manchester City for the sale of Sterling.

Goals of the Season 2014/15

Here's ten crackers from last year's campaign with our ratings out of five for importance and technique...

10 **09** **08** **07** **06**

SAMIR NASRI
V ROMA
(December)

Importance:
*****

Technique:
****

When City needed something special, Samir Nasri delivered the goods with a stunning goal away to Roma. The midfielder picked up the ball 30 yards out, cut inside, and unleashed a fearsome drive from the edge of the box to put the Blues on the way to a vital Champions League win.

YAYA TOURE V
PALACE
(April)

Importance:
***

Technique:
****

Though City were 2-0 down at the time, Yaya Toure's late consolation gave a little hope. The Ivorian picked up the ball on the right of the Palace box before firing a fierce low shot into the bottom corner to halve the deficit. It was too little, too late – but what a goal!

DAVID SILVA
V WEST HAM
(October)

Importance:
****

Technique:
*****

Another game where City found themselves a couple of goals behind to a team they were expected to beat. West Ham were two up with 75 minutes gone. A couple of minutes later, there was a glimmer of hope as David Silva picked the ball up on the left, drifted past three challenges before curling a beautiful shot into the far corner from 18 yards.

EDIN DZEKO
V HULL CITY
(September)

Importance:
***

Technique:
****

City raced out of the blocks away to Hull City and were 2-0 up with just 11 minutes played. Sergio Aguero scored the first on seven minutes and Edin Dzeko doubled the lead just four minutes later, collecting the ball 25 yards out before nudging it to the right of his marker and curling a superb shot into the top right-hand corner.

GAEL CLICHY
V SOUTHAMPTON
(November)

Importance:
****

Technique:
****

Gael Clichy's first ever City goal was a thing of beauty, and a terrific team goal that started in the Blues' own box as Frank Lampard played the ball to Clichy, took a return pass and found Silva who fed Aguero. The Argentinian then played a delightful cross with the outside of his boot and Clichy finished the move with a shot into the roof of the net from six yards.

PABLO ZABALETA
V SUNDERLAND
(December)
Importance:
****

Technique:
****

Not renowned for his goal-scoring perhaps, Pablo Zabaleta took this goal with the coolness of a high-class striker. Made by Samir Nasri who spotted Zabaleta's overlap into the box, the Frenchman played a clever pass behind the defensive line and Zabaleta cleverly dinked the ball over Costel Pantilimon before running off to celebrate in a 'baby's coming soon' style!

SERGIO AGUERO
V TOTTENHAM
(May)
Importance:
****

Technique:
****

The only goal of a tight game. City showed how to counter-attack in devastating fashion when a corner was cleared and the ball found its way to David Silva who played in Aguero who smashed the ball in from 12 yards out. The whole move had taken less than 10 seconds from box-to-box!

SERGIO AGUERO
V SUNDERLAND
(November)
Importance:
****

Technique:
****

City had gone behind to Connor Wickham's early goal, but Aguero brought City level with a devastating finish. He received the ball 30 yards from goal, pushed it forward with electric pace and through the legs of a defender before hitting a shot past Pantilimon that was so powerful it almost broke the net.

JAMES MILNER
V STOKE
(February)
Importance:
***

Technique:
****

A superb team goal and the only header in the list, James Milner put City 3-1 up away to Stoke. Silva and Nasri worked their way out of a tight corner with some sublime skill and Nasri's pinpoint cross into the box allowed Milner to merely direct the ball, using the pace of the cross to give the keeper no chance.

SAMIR NASRI
v Stoke
(February)
Importance:
***

Technique:
****

Another goal against the Potters. This was a well-deserved strike from man-of-the-match Nasri. He ran towards the Stoke penalty area at pace, glided past one challenge, and feigned a shot before unleashing a drive that ended in the bottom corner of the net from 20 yards, completing a 4-1 win and a rare success away to Stoke.

WIN A SIGNED CITY 2015/16 SHIRT!

Fancy owning a new City shirt signed by all your favourite players?

Answer the following question to be in with a chance:

Which club did Kevin De Bruyne join City from?

A) Werder-Bremen
B) Wolfsberg
C) Bayern Munich

Entry is by email only. One entry per contestant. Please enter MCFC SHIRT followed by either A, B or C in the subject line of an email. In the body of the email, please include your name, address, postcode, email address and phone number and send to: frontdesk@grangecommunications.co.uk by Friday 25 March 2016.

Wordsearch#1

See how many City-related words you can find in our Wordsearch and remember the words could be horizontal, vertical or diagonal!

```
O  M  E  R  U  O  T  N  N  K  V  A
H  M  R  N  O  C  X  B  Y  L  T  H
N  N  Y  M  C  D  B  L  O  E  K  R
I  X  N  A  L  K  N  Z  L  N  F  Y
D  K  A  N  Q  D  R  A  N  L  Y  Z
N  N  P  G  P  Q  B  C  N  N  B  K
A  D  M  A  K  A  L  K  G  R  K  Z
N  T  O  L  Z  S  H  X  K  R  E  T
R  F  K  A  I  M  W  B  Q  F  R  F
E  N  X  L  T  H  F  T  D  A  X  L
F  Y  V  N  D  Q  V  Y  H  H  K  B
R  A  D  E  M  I  C  H  E  L  I  S
```

Vincent Kompany
Pablo Zabaleta
Martin Demichelis
Fernandinho

Wilfried Bony
Eliaquim Mangala
David Silva
Yaya Toure

Fernando
Joe Hart

Answers on page 60&61

Guess who?

Here are four mystery City players – use your powers of observation and detective work to solve their identity....

WHO'S THE ENQUIRING MIND AT THE SHOOT?

WRAPPING UP FOR THE COLD – BUT WHO IS IT?

Answers on page 60&61

C

SPLASH DOWN! BUT WHO ARE
THESE TWO CITY STARS?

D

ICE BUCKET CHALLENGE
– BUT CAN YOU FIGURE
OUT WHO IS GETTING A
SOAKING?

BREAKING THROUGH

Four exciting players to watch out for during 2015/16 season...

BRANDON BARKER: WINGER

Exciting winger Brandon Barker was one of the shining lights of Patrick Vieira's Elite Development Squad during 2014/15. Comfortable with either foot, Barker can switch wings and torment both full-backs with equal effectiveness. A Manchester boy, Barker is expected to either push for a senior squad role this season or perhaps spend time out on loan to gain more experience.

KELECHI IHEANACHO: STRIKER

Nigerian striker Kelechi Iheanacho has already made quite an impression on the City fans. The talented teenager played for the first team during the 2014 summer tour of the USA, and he scored a couple of goals as well as showing some skilful touches. Injury kept him out for several months last season, but he returned towards the end of the campaign to score a couple of excellent goals. Kelechi has genuine promise and is expected to challenge for a regular place in the senior squad during 2015/16.

JASON DENAYER: DEFENDER

Belgian defender Jason Denayer made excellent progress during a year-long loan with Celtic in 2014/15, where he played 44 times and was voted the Scottish PFA Player of the Year and the Celtic Young Player of the Year after a superb season for the Hoops. Denayer also won three full Belgium caps. Jason joined Galatasaray on loan for the 2015/16 season.

MANU GARCIA: MIDFIELDER

One of the brightest young stars to emerge through the Club's ranks in recent years, Spanish play-maker Manu Garcia was impressive throughout the 2014/15 campaign and City's 2015 summer tour. The diminutive play-maker joined the Blues from Sporting Gijon in 2014 and his range of passing and vision has made him one of the EDS' most promising prospects. Manager Manuel Pellegrini started the 17-year-old in four of the Blues' five summer friendlies, clearly impressed by Manu's progress. Definitely one to watch.

Crossword

Can you solve the MCFC Annual Crossword 2016? It gets easier the more you answers you fill in!

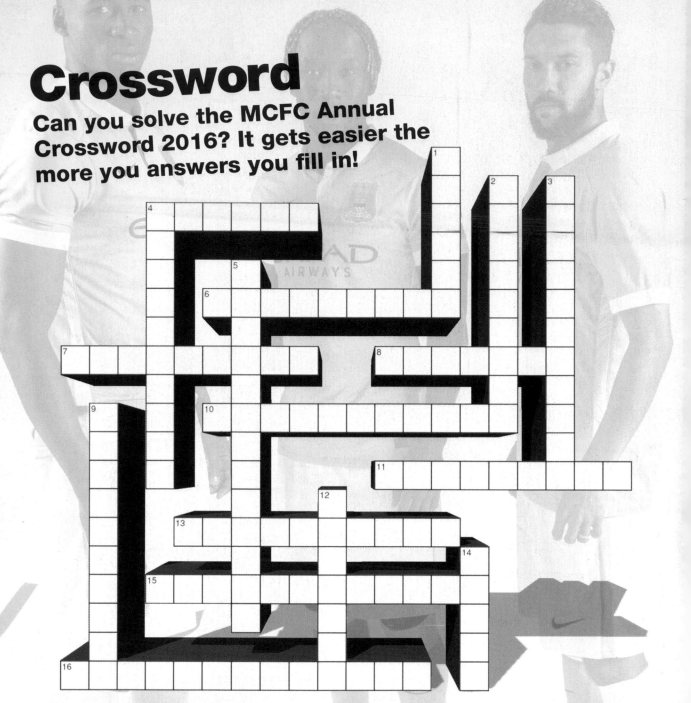

ACROSS

1. Who was City's top scorer last season? (6, 6)
2. From which team did Fernando sign? (5)
3. Which club did Matija Nastasic leave City for? (7)
4. Joe Hart saved a penalty against this Barcelona superstar. (6, 5)
5. City played Arsenal at Wembley at the start of the 2014/15 season – what shield were they playing for? (9)
6. Which was the first team to beat City at home last season? (5, 4)
7. Vincent Kompany plays international football for this country. (7)
8. This team knocked City out of the FA Cup. (12)
9. Which Sheffield club did City draw in both the FA Cup and the Capital One Cup? (9)
10. City loaned John Guidetti to this Scottish club last season? (6)

DOWN

11. The team Frank Lampard left City for. (3, 4, 4)
12. Wilfried Bony and Yaya Toure represent which country? (5, 5)
13. The head coach of City's EDS team? (7, 6)
14. City left this training ground last season to move to the CFA (10)
15. Micah Richards signed for this club in July 2015? (5, 5)
16. Which country does Fernandinho play for? (6)
17. James Milner left City for who? (9)
18. The team Sergio Aguero scored his 100th City goal against? (10, 6)
19. The team that beat City in the FA Youth Cup final (7)
20. Which team from City's Champions League group eventually won the competition? (9)

Answers on page 60&61

RAHEEM STERLING

Spot the Ball#1

See if you can figure out where the ball is in the picture below? Use Vincent's body language a clue

Answers on page 60&61

Kings of Social Media

Here are City players with the most followers on Twitter...

NASRI:
2,582,527

SILVA:
3,368,038

KOMPANY:
2,229,076

AGUERO:
8,733,713

ZABALETA:
2,124,569

STERLING:
1,218,877

YAYA:
134,895

FERNANDINHO:
1,073,373

NAVAS:
227,731

SAGNA:
747,211

AS OF AUGUST 2015, THESE WERE THE TOP MCFC 10 PLAYERS ON TWITTER...

Answers on page 60&61

KEVIN DE BRUYNE

Kevin De Bruyne became City's record signing when he joined from VfL Wolfsburg

Regarded as one of the best young attacking midfielders in Europe, Kevin De Bruyne will add a new dimension to City's attack this season.

A fabulous 2014/15 season saw the Belgian international pick up the Bundesliga Player of the Year award after an impressive tally of 21 assists for VfL Wolfsburg in all competitions, a new record for the German Division and higher than any Premier League player last year, as well as landing the Footballer of the Year in Germany award.

His tremendous contribution helped Wolfsburg finish second in the Bundesliga behind Bayern Munich, meaning they automatically qualified for this season's UEFA Champions League Group Stage. De Bruyne also started and scored in the club's historic 2015 DFB-Pokal Final 3-1 victory over Borussia Dortmund at the Olympiastadion in Berlin to win the tournament for the very first time.

His wide range of passing and long-range shooting meant he was the main creative output for Wolfsburg last year with 111 chances created in total, more than any current City player.

He began his career at Belgium side Genk, where he scored 15 goals in 72 appearances between 2008 and 2012. In that time he won the Belgian Pro League (2010-11) Belgian Cup (2008-09) and the Belgian Supercup (2011).

This won't be the first outing in the Premier League for De Bruyne, after a short spell for Chelsea when the midfielder made a £7 million pound move switch from Gent in January 2012 on deadline day.

He was loaned out to Werder Bremen for the 2012/13 season where he scored 10 goals and won the Bundesliga Young Player of the Year before returning to Stanford Bridge.

His beautifully weighted pass into Oscar's path helped Chelsea ease to a 2-0 win at home to Hull on the opening day of the 2013/14 season, but despite an impressive start, that was to be his only assist for the club as his chances of action were limited with just three league appearances in total.

On 18 January 2014, Wolfsburg signed De Bruyne for a fee of £18million and he hit the ground running with a goal in Wolfsburg's 3-1 away win at Hamburger SV just a week later.

He's made a big impression on the international stage too, with De Bruyne becoming a regular member of Belgium's team during the 2014 FIFA World Cup qualification campaign where he scored four goals en route to his country's first major tournament in 12 years.

He was named in Belgium's squad for the 2014 FIFA World Cup, was the supplier for Marouane Fellaini's equaliser in their first game of the tournament against Algeria and was named man of the match by FIFA. In the round of 16, De Bruyne scored Belgium's opening goal in the third minute of extra time as they defeated the United States 2–1.

Now he returns to England with a determination to show Chelsea what they missed out on. His link-up in midfield with the likes of David Silva and new signing Raheem Sterling will be one to watch out for as Pellegrini's attacking options reach new levels.

Name: Kevin De Bruyne
Position: Attacking Midfielder, Winger
Squad number: 17
Date of birth: 28/06/1991
Previous clubs: Genk, Chelsea, Genk (loan), Werder Bremen (loan), VfL Wolfsburg
2014/15 Apps (All Comps) 51 starts (for VfL Wolfsburg)
2014/15 Goals (All Comps): 16
2014/15 Assists (All Comps): 28

THE BIG
CITY QUIZ 2016

25 questions to test your City knowledge... award yourself a point for each correct answer but some carry extra bonus points for difficulty – there's a total of 50 points   available!

01 Who scored City's last goal of the 2014/15 season?

02 True or false? City began and ended the 2014/15 Premier League season with the same score – name the teams and score-line
(3 bonus points)

03 How many goals did Sergio Aguero score in all competitions last season?
(+2 bonus points)

04 Which club did Jason Denayer spend the 2014/15 season on loan with?

05 How many Golden Glove awards has Joe Hart now won? 1,3 or 4 (+2 bonus points)

06 True or False? Jesus Navas joined City from Osasuna (+1 bonus point)

07 Who wears these boots? (+2 bonus points)

15 Which three City players played in the 2014 World Cup Final? (+ 3 bonus points)

16 Which team did Micah Richards spend a season on loan with?

17 True or false? Sergio Aguero has never been included in the PFA Team of the Season.

18 Which competition did the EDS win last season? (+ 2 bonus points)

22 Which country does promising striker Kelechi Iheanacho represent? (+2 bonus points)

23 Who scored their first ever City goal in the 3-0 win at Southampton last season?

24 Sergio Aguero scored a penalty after just two minutes against which club last season?

08 Who knocked City out of the Capital One Cup?

09 Which team did Marcos Lopes join on a permanent deal in August 2015? (+2 bonus points)

10 Which was City's only Champions League away win last season?

11 Which two City players were sent off against CSKA Moscow? (+ 2 bonus points)

12 Who did Sergio Aguero score four goals against in one game last season?

13 Which club did Alvaro Negredo join on a permenant deal from.

14 Which team did Eliaquim Mangala concede a penalty and score an own goal against? (+1 bonus point)

19 Who scored all City's goals against Manchester United, home and away, last season?

20 Which is the only team Frank Lampard scored against both home and away? (+2 bonus points)

21 Which appearance landmark did Joe Hart pass last season? 100, 200 or 300 games?

25 How many goals did David Silva score in 2014/15? (+1 bonus point)

SCORE CHART:

50-41 points:
Manager of the Year - and a job for life

40-31 :
The board would like to extend your contract by two years

30-21:
Your job is safe for another season – the board issue as vote of confidence

20-11:
The board would like a chat...

10-0:
Relegation form – you're sacked!

Answers on page 60&61

New Signing #3
NICOLAS OTAMENDI

Argentina star Nicolas Otamendi brings with him a wealth of La Liga and international experiences...

Nicolas Otamendi joined City during the summer transfer window and in doing so became one of Europe's most expensive defenders. The Argentine international opted for the No.30 shirt and is set to challenge Vincent Kompany, Eliaquim Mangala and Martin Demichelis for a starting place in the Blues' defence.

Recognised as one of the continent's best central defenders, Otamendi left Valencia where his performances earned him a place in La Liga's 2014/15 Team of the Season. In the summer, the 27-year old was a teammate of Sergio Aguero, Martin Demichelis and Pablo Zabaleta as Argentina reached the Copa America final. Although Argentina were defeated by Chile on penalties, Nicolas was recognised for his excellent form throughout the competition with a place in the Team of the Tournament as his side conceded just three goals in their six games. Speaking shortly after arriving, Otamendi said, "I am here to give my best, to fight game by game and push City to the highest peaks for as long as possible, and I hope we will be able to win several cups and titles.

That's the most important. To be here inside a club that looks so wonderful from the outside is a dream." Otamendi's signing reunites Fernando and Eliaquim Mangala with their former FC Porto teammate.

Nicolas won the Primeira Liga three times in his four years in Portugal, as well as the Europa League and the Portuguese Cup in 2011.

The Buenos Aires-born man started out his career at Velez Sarsfield where he spent 15 years between 1995 and 2010. During this 15-year association with Velez, Otamendi brought the 2009 Clausura to the Jose Amalfitani Stadium and was named in the 2009 South American Team of the Year – just one year after his senior debut in May 2008.

Earning his first senior international call-up from Diego Maradona in qualifiers for the 2010 World Cup, Nicolas made his debut against Panama as a 19-year old in a 3-1 win. He has since gone on play 25 times for his nation, representing them in the 2010 World Cup.

Name: Nicolas Otamendi
Squad number: 30

Date of birth: 12/02/1988
Place of birth: Buenos Aires

Previous clubs: Velez Sarsfield, Porto Valencia, Athletico Mineiro (Loan)

Total City career: 0
International caps: 25

New Signing #4
PATRICK ROBERTS

Exciting England Under-19 winger Patrick Roberts joined City in the summer having signed from Fulham.

Signed with his potential in mind, Roberts will hope to see some first team football this season, but is more likely to feature for the Elite Development Squad or even be loaned out to another club to gain vital senior experience.

Rated as one of the most exciting young talents to emerge in the last couple of years, the West London-born teenager started his youth career with AFC Wimbledon before moving to Fulham at the age of 13.

He made his Fulham Premier League debut against City in March 2014, and was the driving force behind Fulham's run to the FA Youth Cup where they were eventually beaten by Chelsea.

Labelled the 'English Messi' by some writers in the media, Roberts has excellent technique, balance and dribbling ability. His former Fulham manager Felix Magath described him as "an extraordinary talent" and it was reported that Chelsea and Liverpool were also keen to sign him.

He made his City debut on the Australian pre-season tour, replacing Jesus Navas, against Real Madrid no less!

He has so far represented England at Under 16, 17 and 19 levels and is expected to continue his progression in the coming months. An exciting prospect, he will wear the No.27 shirt for City.

Name: Patrick Roberts
Position: Winger
Squad Number: 27

Date of Birth: 05/02/1997
Previous Clubs: Fulham

2014/15 Apps (All Comps): 20 starts (for Fulham)
2014/15 Goals (All Comps): 0
Total City career: 0
Played: 0, Goals: 0

Spot the Difference

Can you spot the 5 differences between picture A and picture B as Fabian Delph gets into shape? Circle as many as you can!

Where's Zaba?

There's a Poznan going down, and somewhere in the crowd of City fans is Pablo Zabaleta - can you spot him?

KELECHI IHEANACHO

MCFC 42

Wordsearch#2

Find the words in the grid. Words can go horizontally, vertically and diagonally in all eight directions.

A T T J Y K L X P E V F
W N H B Q D M R I P E L
A Y M J Y A O P T M R O
Y S Z L S G I S D R A O
F X C C R T X Y W R U D
A Z O A L Q L O X J Q L
N T M A R G N B Y X S I
S M B K F F F L T N Y G
E X N L J Q V L Q V T H
S C O R E B O A R D I T
Y X N V D C Y B D F C S
R E T S E H C N O O M M

AwayFans   Floodlights   Scarf
Ballboys   Mascots   Scoreboard
BaltiPie   Moonchester
CitySquare   Programme

Answers on page 60&61

Spot the Ball

Can you figure out where the ball is in the picture above? Select your grid reference and see how accurate you've been...

Answers on page 60&61

Text 4 Who?

Four mobile phones were left in the changing rooms. To reunite the phone with their owner, we've opened the last text message they received. Can you figure out who we should give which phone to?

That's four times you've won that award now! And congrats on reaching 300 appearances, big man!

Great season! And you've played even better without the ponytail!

Great work beating Kane and Costa to the top of the list! Enjoy the boot!

Can you make a rabbit appear out of a hat, too? Just magic, mate!

Answers on page 60&61

New Signing #5
FABIAN DELPH

Fabian Delph joined City from Aston Villa to add extra bite into the Blues' midfield engine room.

Having established himself as an integral member of the Aston Villa side where he had also taken on the Captain's armband, Delph decided that the chance to play for the Blues was too good an opportunity to turn down. No doubt the combative midfielder will bring plenty of vim and vigour to the City squad as his career continues a steep upward curve. The Blues paid £8m for his services – the activation fee in his contract – though he is valued at a much higher price on the open market.

By the time Delph joined City in July 2015 he'd also become a regular member of Roy Hodgson's England squad, winning six caps during the 2014/15 campaign and pressing for inclusion at the 2016 European Championships.

He will wear the No.18 shirt for City and has promised to 'work his socks off' for the Blues in the coming years.

Delph began his senior career at Leeds United, making 50 appearances between 2006 and 2009.

In 2009 he was voted the Leeds United Young Player of the Year and Leeds United Players' Player of the Year. He was also named in the PFA League One Team of the Year as well as winning the Football League Player of the Year to cap a memorable campaign for the Lilywhites.

Widely regarded as one of the brightest talents outside the Premier League, he moved to Aston Villa in 2009 for an undisclosed fee aged just 19.

He initially found it hard to nail down a regular starting role at Villa, and had a brief spell back on loan with Leeds United in 2012 before finally establishing himself at Villa Park during the 2012/13 campaign.

Thereafter, he became an integral member of the first team, and was voted the club's Player of the Year in 2013/14. Having represented England at Under-19 and Under-21 level, he won his first full cap against Norway in September 2014. After signing a new deal with the Midlands outfit in January 2015, he was handed the Captain's armband by new manager Tim Sherwood.

Delph made 128 appearances for Villa, scoring eight goals.

Name: Fabian Delph
Position: Midfielder
Squad Number: 18

Date of Birth: 21/11/1989
Previous Clubs: Leeds United, Aston Villa, (Leeds United loan)

2014/15 Apps (All Comps): 26 starts (for Villa)
2014/15 Goals (All Comps): 2
Total City career: 0
Played: 0, Goals: 0

NAME: JOE HART
POSITION: GOALKEEPER
SQUAD NUMBER: 1

DATE OF BIRTH: 19/04/1987
PREVIOUS CLUBS:
SHREWSBURY, TRANMERE ROVERS
(LOAN), BLACKPOOL (LOAN),
BIRMINGHAM CITY (LOAN)

2014/15 APPS (ALL COMPS):
43 STARTS
2014/15 GOALS (ALL COMPS):
0
TOTAL CITY CAREER:
PLAYED: 300 GOALS: 0

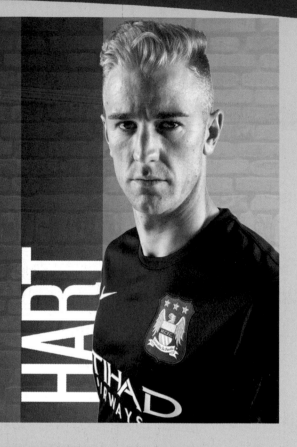

NAME: WILLY CABALLERO
POSITION: GOALKEEPER
SQUAD NUMBER: 13

DATE OF BIRTH: 13/05/1983
PREVIOUS CLUBS: BOCA
JUNIORS, ELCHE, ARSENAL
SARANDI (LOAN), MALAGA

2014/15 APPS (ALL COMPS):
7 STARTS
2014/15 GOALS (ALL COMPS):
0
TOTAL CITY CAREER:
PLAYED: 7 GOALS: 0

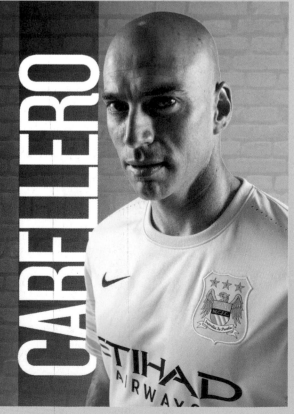

NAME: GAËL CLICHY
POSITION: LEFT-BACK
SQUAD NUMBER: 22

DATE OF BIRTH: 26/07/1985
PREVIOUS CLUBS: CANNES,
ARSENAL

2014/15 APPS (ALL COMPS):
30 STARTS + 1 SUB
2014/15 GOALS (ALL COMPS):
1
TOTAL CITY CAREER:
PLAYED: 126 (+10 SUB) GOALS: 1

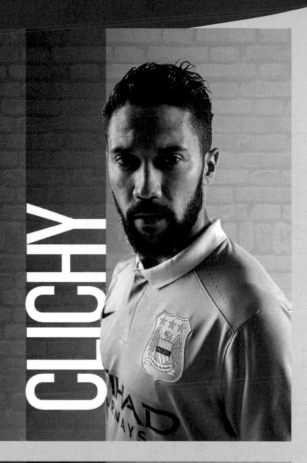

CLICHY

NAME: ALEKSANDAR KOLAROV
POSITION: LEFT-BACK
SQUAD NUMBER: 11

DATE OF BIRTH: 10/11/1985
PREVIOUS CLUBS: CUKARICKI,
OFK BEOGRAD, LAZIO

2014/15 APPS (ALL COMPS):
23 STARTS +7 SUB
2014/15 GOALS (ALL COMPS):
2
TOTAL CITY CAREER:
PLAYED: 122 (46) GOALS: 17

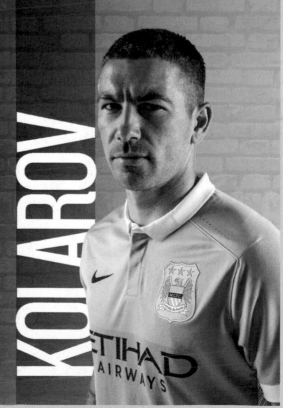

KOLAROV

NAME: PABLO ZABALETA
POSITION: RIGHT-BACK
SQUAD NUMBER: 5

DATE OF BIRTH: 16/01/1985
PREVIOUS CLUBS: SAN LORENZO, ESPANYOL

2014/15 APPS (ALL COMPS):
35 STARTS +1 SUB
2014/15 GOALS (ALL COMPS):
2
TOTAL CITY CAREER:
PLAYED: 246 (33) GOALS: 10

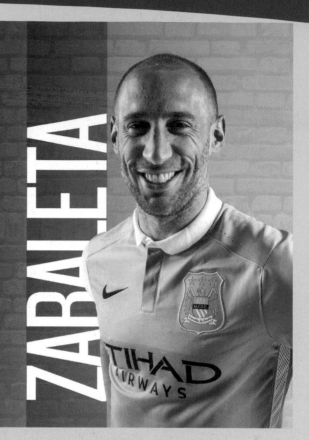

ZABALETA

NAME: BACARY SAGNA
POSITION: RIGHT-BACK
SQUAD NUMBER: 3

DATE OF BIRTH: 14/02/1983
PREVIOUS CLUBS: AUXERRE, ARSENAL

2014/15 APPS (ALL COMPS):
14 STARTS +2 SUB
2014/15 GOALS (ALL COMPS):
0
TOTAL CITY CAREER:
PLAYED: 14 (+2) GOALS: 0

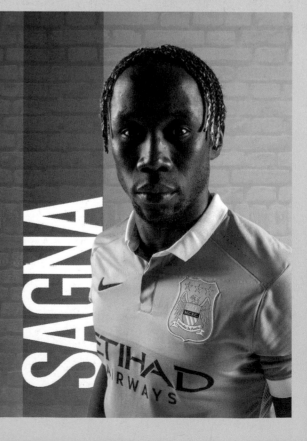

SAGNA

NAME: ELIAQUIM MANGALA
POSITION: CENTRE-BACK
SQUAD NUMBER: 20

DATE OF BIRTH:
PREVIOUS CLUBS: STANDARD
LIEGE, PORTO B, PORTO

2014/15 APPS (ALL COMPS):
30 STARTS +1 SUB
2014/15 GOALS (ALL COMPS):
0
TOTAL CITY CAREER:
PLAYED: 30 (+1SUB) GOALS: 0

MANGALA

NAME: MARTIN DEMICHELIS
POSITION: CENTRE-BACK
SQUAD NUMBER: 26

DATE OF BIRTH: 20/12/1980
PREVIOUS CLUBS: RIVER PLATE,
BAYERN MUNICH, MALAGA,
ATLETICO MADRID

2014/15 APPS (ALL COMPS):
36 STARTS+ 4 SUB
2014/15 GOALS (ALL COMPS):
1
TOTAL CITY CAREER:
PLAYED: 70 (+5) GOALS: 3

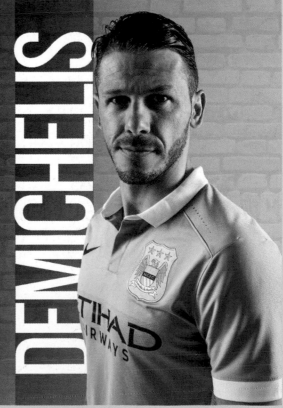

DEMICHELIS

NAME: VINCENT KOMPANY (CAPTAIN)
POSITION: CENTRE-BACK
SQUAD NUMBER: 4

DATE OF BIRTH: 10/04/1986
PREVIOUS CLUBS: ANDERLECHT, SV HAMBURG

2014/15 APPS (ALL COMPS):
31 STARTS +2 SUB
2014/15 GOALS (ALL COMPS):
0
TOTAL CITY CAREER:
PLAYED: 265 (+11) GOALS: 12

KOMPANY

NAME: JESUS NAVAS
POSITION: ATTACKING MIDFIELDER
SQUAD NUMBER: 15

DATE OF BIRTH: 21/11/1985
PREVIOUS CLUBS: SEVILLA

2014/15 APPS (ALL COMPS):
32 STARTS +15 SUB
2014/15 GOALS (ALL COMPS):
1
TOTAL CITY CAREER:
PLAYED: 61 (+34 SUB) GOALS: 7

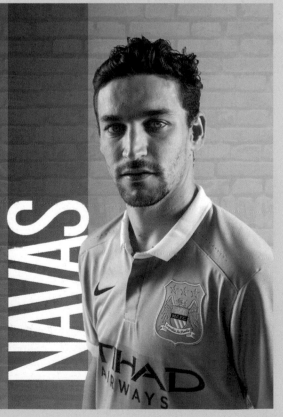

NAVAS

NAME: NICOLAS OTAMENDI
POSITION: CENTRAL DEFENDER
SQUAD NUMBER: 30

DATE OF BIRTH: 12/02/1988
PREVIOUS CLUBS: VELEZ SARSFIELD, PORTO, VALENCIA, ATLETICO MINEIRO (LOAN)

APPEARANCES (FOR VALENCIA): 38

2014/15 APPS (ALL COMPS): 35

2014/15 GOALS: 6 (ALL COMPS)

INTERNATIONAL CAPS: 25* AS AT 1 SEPTEMBER 2015

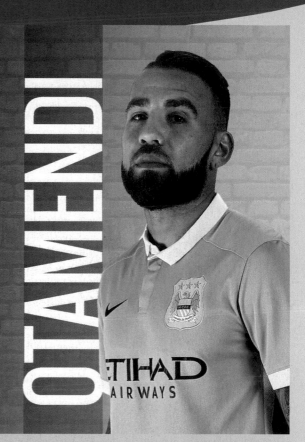

NAME: FERNANDO
POSITION: CENTRAL MIDFIELD
SQUAD NUMBER: 6

DATE OF BIRTH: 25/07/1987
PREVIOUS CLUBS: VILA NOVA, ESTRELA AMADORA (LOAN), PORTO

2014/15 APPS (ALL COMPS): 30 STARTS, +3 SUB
2014/15 GOALS (ALL COMPS): 2
TOTAL CITY CAREER: PLAYED: 30 (+3 SUB) GOALS: 2

NAME: FERNANDINHO
POSITION: CENTRAL MIDFIELD
SQUAD NUMBER: 25

DATE OF BIRTH: 04/05/1985
PREVIOUS CLUBS: ATLETICO PARANAENSE, SHAKHTAR DONETSK

2014/15 APPS (ALL COMPS):
31 + 12 SUB
2014/15 GOALS (ALL COMPS):
2
TOTAL CITY CAREER:
PLAYED: 73 (+16) GOALS: 8

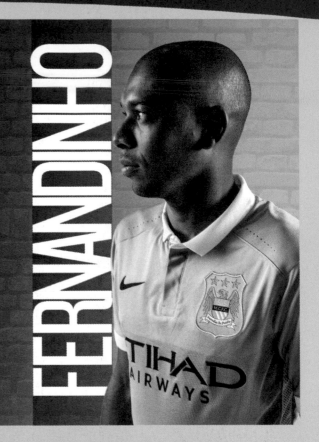

FERNANDINHO

NAME: SAMIR NASRI
POSITION: ATTACKING MIDFIELD
SQUAD NUMBER: 8

DATE OF BIRTH: 26/06/1987
PREVIOUS CLUBS: MARSEILLE, ARSENAL

2014/15 APPS (ALL COMPS):
24 + 9 SUB
2014/15 GOALS (ALL COMPS):
3
TOTAL CITY CAREER:
PLAYED: 131 (+32) GOALS: 25

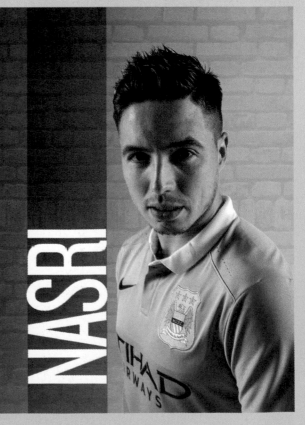

NASRI

NAME: YAYA TOURÉ
POSITION: CENTRAL MIDFIELD
SQUAD NUMBER: 42

DATE OF BIRTH: 13/05/1983
PREVIOUS CLUBS: SK BEVEREN, METALURH DONETSK, OLYMPIACOS, MONACO, BARCELONA

2014/15 APPS (ALL COMPS):
36 STARTS +2 SUB
2014/15 GOALS (ALL COMPS):
12
TOTAL CITY CAREER:
PLAYED: 214 (+7 SUB) GOALS: 67

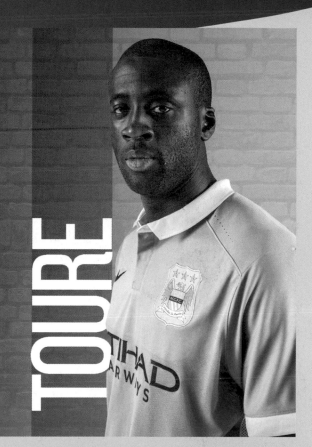

NAME: DAVID SILVA
POSITION: ATTACKING MIDFIELD
SQUAD NUMBER: 21

DATE OF BIRTH: 08/01/1986
PREVIOUS CLUBS: VALENCIA, EIBAR (LOAN), CELTA VIGO (LOAN)

2014/15 APPS (ALL COMPS):
39 + 3 SUB
2014/15 GOALS (ALL COMPS):
12
TOTAL CITY CAREER:
PLAYED: 202 (+23) GOALS: 39

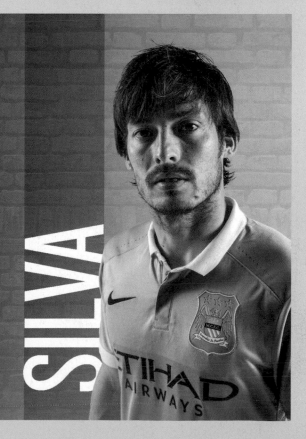

NAME: WILFRIED BONY
POSITION: STRIKER
SQUAD NUMBER: 14

DATE OF BIRTH: 10/12/88
PREVIOUS CLUBS: ISSIA WAZI,
SPARTA PRAGUE, VITESSE,
SWANSEA

2014/15 APPS (ALL COMPS):
2 +10
2014/15 GOALS (ALL COMPS):
2
TOTAL CITY CAREER:
PLAYED: 2 (+10) GOALS: 2

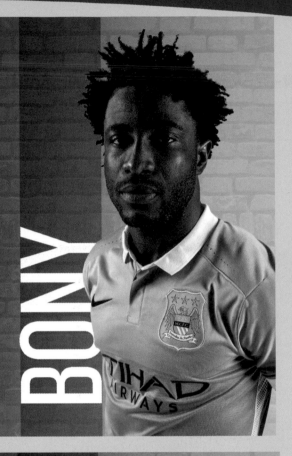

BONY

NAME: SERGIO AGÜERO
POSITION: STRIKER
SQUAD NUMBER: 16
DATE OF BIRTH: 02/06/1988
PREVIOUS CLUBS:
INDEPENDIENTE, ATLÉTICO MADRID

2014/15 APPS (ALL COMPS):
37 +5 SUB
2014/15 GOALS (ALL COMPS):
32
TOTAL CITY CAREER:
PLAYED: 136 (+28) GOALS: 107

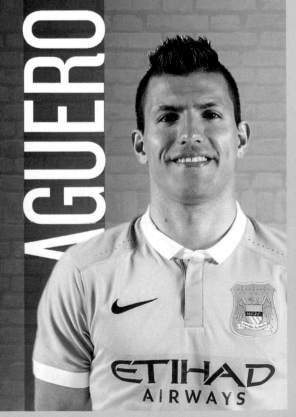

AGUERO

MCFC PLAYER OF THE YEAR 2014/15:

SERGIO AGUERO

Sergio Aguero was voted City's Etihad Player of the Year (in association with the Official Supporters Club) for the 2014/15 campaign.

Kun won the award after yet another superb season for the Blues, during which he bagged 32 goals in all competitions and won the Premier League's Golden Boot.

It's the second time he has won the award, with his 30-goal haul during the 2011/12 title-winning campaign helping him to the prize – an honour that has now gone to an Argentinian for four of the past six seasons. Carlos Tevez and Pablo Zabaleta won the vote in 2010 and 2013 respectively.

Joe Hart was voted runner-up and David Silva – a constant name on the shortlist – came third. Hart and Raheem Sterling will be hoping to become the first English players to take the prize since Shaun Wright-Phillips in 2004. Michael Brown is the only other English name since 1995.

Richard Dunne remains the record-holder of Player of the Year awards for the Blues, with the Irish defender winning four consecutive votes from 2005-2008. Joe Corrigan is the only player to have won more than twice after receiving the prize in 1976, 1978 and 1980.

DAVID
SILVA

FERNANDINHO

QuizAnswers

WORDSEARCH#1
(From page 23)

```
O M E R U O T N N K V A
H M R N O C X B Y L T H
N N Y M C D B L O E K R
I X N A L K N Z L N F Y
D K A N Q D R A N L Y Z
N N P G P Q B C N N B K
A D M A K A L K G R K Z
N T O L Z S H X K R E T
R F K A I M W B Q F R F
E N X L T H F T D A X L
F Y V N D Q V Y H H K B
R A D E M I C H E L I S
```

GUESS WHO?
(From page 24)

A Aguero

B Kompany

C Kompany & Hart

D Nasri

CROSSWORD#1
(From page 28)

```
CELTIC        BRAZIL  COMMUNITY  LIONEL
CARRINGTON    M                  MESS
  LIVERPOOL   I                  MESS
WEDNESDAY     D       BELGIUM    MESS
  NEWYORKCITY L                  MESS
              E                  MESS
ASTON     NEWYORKCITY  STOKECITY
VILL  IVORYCOAST           PORTO
  SERGIOAGUERO            PORTO
PATRICKVIEIRA            PORTO
```

THE BIG CITY QUIZ - ANSWERS
(From page 34&35)

01, SERGIO AGUERO	15, MARTIN DEMICHELIS, SERGIO AGUERO, AND PABLO ZABALETA
02, TRUE – 2-0 V NEWCASTLE AND SOUTHAMPTON	
	16, FIORENTINA
03, 32	
	17, TRUE – HE HASN'T FEATURED IN ANY OF THE FOUR PFA TEAMS HE QUALIFIED FOR
04, CELTIC	
05, 4	18, PREMIER LEAGUE INTERNATIONAL CUP
06, FALSE – SEVILLA	
07, SERGIO AGUERO	19, SERGIO AGUERO
08, NEWCASTLE	20, SOUTHAMPTON
09, MONACO	21, 300
10, ROMA	22, NIGERIA
11, FERNANDINHO AND YAYA TOURE	23, GAEL CLICHY
12, TOTTENHAM	24, WEST BROM
13, VALENCIA	25, 12
14, HULL CITY	AWARD YOURSELF ONE POINT UNLESS STATED!

SPOT THE BALL#1
(From page 30)

SPOT THE DIFFERENCE?
(From page 30)

1, No TV screen on wall at back
2, No number on shorts
3, No Matrix sign on bike (logo)
4, No signage on glass window
5, Yellow wall at back

TEXT 4 WHO?
(From page 45)

THAT'S FOUR TIMES YOU'VE WON THAT AWARD NOW! AND CONGRATS ON REACHING 300 APPEARANCES, BIG MAN!
(JOE HART)

GREAT SEASON! AND YOU'VE PLAYED EVEN BETTER WITHOUT THE PONYTAIL!
(MARTIN DEMICHELIS)

GREAT WORK BEATING KANE AND COSTA TO THE TOP OF THE LIST! ENJOY THE BOOT!
(SERGIO AGUERO)

CAN YOU MAKE A RABBIT APPEAR OUT OF A HAT, TOO? JUST MAGIC, MATE!
(DAVID SILVA)

WORDSEARCH#2
(From page 43)

```
A T T J Y K L X P E V F
W N H B Q D M R I P E L
A Y M J Y A O P T M R O
Y S Z L S G I S D R A O
F X C C R T X Y W R U D
A Z O A L Q L O X J Q L
N T M A R G N B Y X S I
S M B K F F L T N Y G G
E X N L J Q V L Q V T H
S C O R E B O A R D I T
Y X N V D C Y B D F C S
R E T S E H C N O O M M
```

SPOT THE BALL#2
(From page 44)

S Recruiting experts worldwide   hays.com

WHERE'S PABLO?
(From page 62)